That Shining Place

That Shining Place

NEW POEMS BY MARK VAN DOREN

 Hill and Wang · *New York*

SOME OF THE POEMS in this volume were previously published as follows: "Truth Is Patient" in *The Antioch Review;* "Birds in the Morning" and "Winter Calligraphy" in the *Chicago Tribune;* "Psalms" in *Columbia Forum;* "Merton's Woods" (under the title "St. Mary's Hermitage, Gethsemani") in *Monk's Pond;* "So Fair a World It Was" in *The Nation;* and "King Wind," "Looking for Something Lost," "Slowly, Slowly Wisdom Gathers," "Wait Till Then," "What Now?" and "Will You, Won't You?" in *Poetry.*

Composed in Granjon types, printed, and bound by American Book–Stratford Press, Inc., New York

To Starr Nelson

Contents

That Shining Place

Slowly, Slowly Wisdom Gathers

Slowly, slowly wisdom gathers:
Golden dust in the afternoon,
Somewhere between the sun and me,
Sometimes so near that I can see,
Yet never settling, late or soon.

Would that it did, and a rug of gold
Spread west of me a mile or more:
Not large, but so that I might lie
Face up, between the earth and sky,
And know what none has known before.

Then I would tell as best I could
The secrets of that shining place:
The web of the world, how thick, how thin,
How firm, with all things folded in;
How ancient, and how full of grace.

What Now?

While the earth turns,
And the skin of it—O, scientist—
Keeps cool, keeps deep;

While the world shines,
And the rind of it—O, radium—
Still does not burn;

While—but why wait?
Don't you hear the dance music,
Old as these hills?

Round with it, round with it,
Stepping, oh, ever so lightly,
Wind in the hair—

What now? You have stopped,
You are weeping. Well, it is difficult,
Dear ones. It is.

So Fair a World It Was

So fair a world it was,
So far away in the dark, the dark,
Yet lighted, oh, so well, so well:
Water and land,
So clear, so sweet;
So fair, it should have been forever.

And would have been, and would have been,
If—what?
Be still. But what?
Keep quiet, child. So fair it was,
The memory is like a death
That dies again; that dies again.

Let Me Go Back

Let me go back to where I began,
If I can find the place.
It was far away and long ago,
And there was a kind of grace
I may not ever,
Having grown old, recover.

I do not even know the time,
Except that it was morning.
It always was; no shadow then
Fell on my soul aborning.
But nights without number
Now are all I remember.

So Idly It Swung

So idly it swung,
That bell in the breeze,
Weightless almost,
And yet it had voice,
So lazily there,
In the answering air,
That tongue in the wind
Sang stories to me.
But when? It has stopped.
But where? I must see,
I must go and find out.
If only I knew
How old I was then,
If only—but listen,
Not that you can,
Now it is talking,
Oh, wonder, again,
As if I were there.
I must tell it I am.

Estote Ergo Vos Perfecti

Be ye therefore perfect.
Be less, and cease to be.
There is no going downward
Save into the great sea
Where things continue falling
Forever and a day;
Except that all is darkness
Down there, O soul of me.

Be ye therefore perfect.
But how shall I do that?
Patience, little brother,
And inwardly take thought.
Breathe evenly. Remember
What many have forgot:
The hill to climb is higher
Even than Ararat.

All of the World at Once

All of the world at once
Called to me. I listened.
But after that, a silence.
It never called again.

Should I have answered,
Saying I was here?
Yet it must have seen me.
And what could I have said?

Shall I say something now?
But why should I presume?
The stillness all around me
Suffices to the end.

Truth Is Patient

Nothing is true that was not true
Before the first man knew it—waiting,
Waiting, not for him, oh, no,
Just waiting, as the cup and saucer
Forgotten on a shelf can wait
Forever to be filled, and no one
Coming, still can wait, still
Be patient. Truth is patient past
The mind's power to measure, past
Is and was, past will be, past
Our knowing, which it no more needs
Than light must have a light to see,
Than love must find excuse to be
What love has been eternally.

Like a Bell in the Night

Like a bell in the night
That nobody sees,
Yet it counts the hours,
And we listen perhaps,
Yet each of us misses
Most of the strokes,

Consequence marches,
Step after step;
Cause, the great king
Who is never at rest,
Couples with change—
This becomes that—

And nobody listens
More than a moment;
Nobody learns
As much as he might
Were time his brother,
Were fate his friend.

Geology

Once on earth there was so much time
There was no time at all;
Or if there was, it was fast and slow
At the same time—O, my soul,

I am dizzy with trying to understand.
Help me, you that can breathe
Time and eternity both, come close
And help me, life in death;

Be here, be there, be now, be then,
And take me with you, O,
My soul that is both fish and man,
That is both yes and no.

Who Was He?

He came to the place at last.
He knew it by one sound:
The talking of old trees.
Nothing but that, but that.

Not to him; to each other.
And yet he understood.
He had not dreamed in vain.
This was the very wood.

The talking never stopped.
And yet no trees were there.
How long ago? And who
Was he to have been told?

He knew by what he could hear.
There was only grass to be seen.
So long ago. But who
Was he to be listening still?

Epitaph for an Infant Buried Long Ago

A ripple in time
Was my short life.
But now the deep stream,
Perfect as ice,

Carries less trace,
Wherever it flows,
Of me and my face
Than eternity does.

Justice, Justice

Solomon and Sancho, wise in judgment,
Knew how to make the truth confess itself:
The child's own mother, seeing the drawn sword,
Surrendered; and the doxy in the ditch
Had muscle to defend her virtue with.

But Solomon and Sancho heard no more
Than two before them, clamoring. What now,
When millions cry? So far away, so faintly,
As if mankind were drowning. Who are the judges
Now, if all are not? And what to do?

If all are not. Ourselves. So what to say?
Justice, justice, where in the swarming world
Do you hide your lovely head? Are you a lady
Still? Or did she die? So faint, so far
The voices sound. Even our own, our own.

No More Buildings

"Tear it down, burn it, blast it."
"Why?" "You fool, for justice." "Good.
Let justice now be everywhere,
Even if all these buildings fall—
Yours, too." "We have no buildings." "So,
No more buildings." "Ours will be—"
"What?" "Temples." "Have a care.
They tumble also, given time."
"Not ours." "Perhaps. But safer yet,
No temples. Nothing. Sun and air
Should be enough for men. Take birds—"
"They build." "Briefly, though, in summer
Air, and then forget." "We can't
Be birds." "No? What a pity." "Only
Builders." "What a waste of stone."

In Winter Sing Summer

In winter sing summer,
In sorrow sing joy;
Not that I mind it—
This bitter day—
But opposite music
Takes longer to die.

Something to keep, then:
A summerlike song
In the middle of blasts
So brutal of tongue,
You would say even silence
Had ceased to sing.

But no, I can hear it:
Warmness in grass,
And wildflowers rising
Where nothing was;
And the sun on my back—ah,
The laziness.

Looking for Something Lost

Looking for something lost is mind
And matter playing a game.
The thing knows it is lost, and waits;
The adversaries are now the same;
The wallet under the leaves
Lies there and breathes.

And what if the something lost was never
Matter in the beginning:
Purpose, or hope, or bravery,
Or innocence, the spirit's cunning?
The piece of the soul that is gone
In the dark shines on.

How to Tell a Story

Take your time.
Tell it slowly.
There is nothing to be gained
By huddling words, by watching me to see
If I grow inattentive; which I shall,
I swear, if you believe I should,
If you have doubts yourself, if you race on
When all I want to have time do is stop
Dead still
So I can be there with you, feeling, seeing.
Start over then and tell your tale
As the clock ticks: Grandfather's clock,
That listens to itself and grins
When we forget to do so; as I would
This hour; which waste for me.
You understand? I want it wasted—
All of it, and not this little bit, my friend,
That in your hurry you already have.

Good News

It was terrible, I tell you,
Waiting to hear the worst;
So that I had no strength left
For—ah, the best.
It came to me and kissed me
Like death, almost.
Then I rejoiced; but faintly,
Like someone lost.

And still I am bruised in places,
Having been saved so late.
The worst had done its wounding
Deep out of sight.
So when shall I recover?
I asked my heart,
Who told me no one ever
Survived such hurt.

No More, No More

How far is it now?
When will there be
No more, no more
Of time or of me?

No telling, I know.
And so I should stop
Wondering how soon
The great weight will drop,

And darkness be all—
Or will there be light,
More of it, more of it,
Blinding my sight

As meteor swift,
As butterfly slow,
Down the deep universe
Dazzled I go?

All Those Lovers

Morning, noon, afternoon, and night,
Someone, somewhere—everywhere—makes love
To someone—oh, the couples of this world
By dark, by day, by sun and moon; or else
No light at all—turn out the light—no, no,
Not yet; well, now; so only the stars—oh, hands
So cunning, and the arms so loose, so loving,
Then finally so tight; the breath that comes,
That goes; the words delicious, or no words
At all, at all—ah, why should there be any?
The lily shoots of April, thrusting up,
Make not one sound, but suddenly are here—
Aha! So all those lovers, secret, silent,
Cover the world; and the world covers them.

Where Were You?

Where were you when I thought the thought—
It is gone now—
Where were you when I said your name,
Which I can no more forget
Than I could lose my way at night across this room
I walk in, walk in, seeing you at the far end
Where of course you never are, having your own
     place,
As I do, in a world I would have made
Less wide, less empty; where I wonder were you
When I thought the thought—what was it?—
When I spoke your name and spiders in their webs
Trembled at the force of it,
And curtains swung,
And the street lights outside my window
Blinked?
And yet it was not loud. And yet I did
Call you. Not as asking you to come, yet I did
Call you. Did you hear?

Never Leave Me

"Never leave me." "No, I won't.
Nor you, either." "No, I'll stay
As long as you do. Then I'll die
The afternoon of that same day."

"Ho, ho!" "I mean it. Not one night
Without you, not one single hour
Even of dusk, that sweetest time
Before the first familiar star."

"The star will miss you." "Not as much
As someone else that knows its name."
"I wonder which one it will be."
"Both will know, if we still dream."

Nosegay for a New Widow

Sadly I bring you
These beautiful daisies;
Open your eyes if you can, for tears,
And see the bright fringes—
Yes, I have told them;
They are your own as long as they last.

Nothing's forever,
Yet perfect in whiteness
These can remind you, oh, my dear,
Of the one you weep for—
Yes, I have told them;
They are for you and nobody else.

Nobody ever
Had such a whiteness
All the way round her; weep, my dear,
And think of these petals—
Yes, I have told them;
Whiter than white, they are yours, they are his.

The World Weighs Nothing

The world weighs nothing.
It is not even air.
Otherwise, beloved,
How terrible to bear:
A great thing on our shoulders
Deforming us the more.

We are not graceful yet.
With luck we may learn to dance.
But what if the world descended
And crushed our only chance?
I think we both would weep then
For how we walked once

And never thought of burdens
Beyond our very own.
Those were enough, beloved,
Together or alone.
And even they, I tell you,
Like yesterday are gone.

The Simplest Words of All

The simplest words of all
Are what I would love you with
Had I an angel's tongue—
Knew the swift sentences
Whereof the world was made
That day before you were.

And yet they made you too:
A whispering, I think,
Between the immense commands
That brought forth day and night.
Would that the world remembered,
And told me, and I spoke.

Until You Come Again

Until you come again,
The world is full of noises
I am past hearing,
Of sights I cannot see.

Until you come again—
Ah, but there you are.
So now they burst upon me,
Those things that were.

Here then is double music,
Of which you are but half,
At least until I hold you
And everything else is still.

To You These Words

To you these words, and may they walk,
Not dance: walk as you do, near the edge
Of dancing, yet not quite. You move
With so controlled a grace, what need
Of music? All the world
Sees how you go there, how you turn and wait,
Then come again, then go. Hears you,
Even, though you make no sound, except
That all things, breathing and unbreathing, follow:
Leave their places when you pass, obedient as liquid
Stirred, as mist on the ground disturbed
And swirling, with no will of its own except
To curl and follow, follow you
Wherever,
Ever.

Valentine

To the other side of the farthest star,
To the outermost dark, then on and on
And on to where pure nothing is—
If that can be, if that can be—
I send your name with a heart around it
To hang on the wall of the world, ah, me.

But only your name. I keep you here
In the innermost quiet of my own mind
Where nothing save pure brightness is—
If that can be, if that can be—
I keep you here with no world round us:
Only your body and mine, ah, me.

Grace on Earth

He was a whole world of wellness.
Birds flew round him wondering
How they might learn more speed,
More joy,
More perfect pitch in singing.

The wind turned and looked back.
He swayed yet did not sway
When it went by him. Such
Lightness, anchored, such
Ease: the very trick of being.

He walked yet did not walk.
The world and he, mutual
In wellness, danced. Yet did not dance;
For he did walk, as waves
Walk, as spring and fall, as wind.

Where is he now, that man?
The grass looks up for him, the trees
Wait, the water in every lake
Listens. Where is that lightfoot
Man, where is he now?

Depression

This day I am cast down,
Cast down. Nothing can stop me
Falling. No one. Don't
Try, or you will go with me.
Where? As if I knew.
No solid ground. This lake,
If it is a lake—it has
No bottom. Things sink
Forever. Yet I'm not wet;
I breathe; so it is air
I drown in. Don't be startled.
I breathe, I say. I even
See—yes, the sun.
But not the same. The back
Side of darkness. Night's
Mirror, silvered. So—
Leave me, please, I am tired.

When I Am Well

When I am well the world is.
All of it learns by speed of light
How happy I am at last, and smiles;
And the butterflies dance higher.

They would dance anyway, but now,
And not to music either, for nothing
Sings, there is scarcely a sound, they lift
And lift as if they would stay there.

Not very long, though; down they tilt
And slip—so wayward, here on flowers,
And there on what?—they settle and work
Their wings; then off, then up

To the top of the house, to the top of the trees,
As if they knew that when I am well
The world is—ho, ho—and the sun
So sweet upon my shoulders.

This Man

(For Archibald MacLeish, at 75)

Nobody, I think, will be there when he comes,
And coming, still walks on, his back so straight,
His voice so beautiful before him, sounding
The unknown dark. O love, O light,
Be with this man forever, be the gifts
That if I had them I would give to him
Who has no need of either love or light,
Being already blessed, this blazing man.

Merton's Woods

The monastery bells can still be heard there.
Or can they? I don't know. I went down once
By the winding path, and all I listened to was trees:
Not huge, but many and high, and busy
With birds; and the top leaves
Twinkled in sun, as did his eyes when he said at
        last,
"Here is my cell." But it was a house,
New-built: a small one, with a porch.
And still I listened to the trees, incessant, sacred:
More than I could count. And acorns dropped,
And squirrels scampered. Foxes too,
He told me, played some days in the distance,
Wary of man—even of him—yet they did caper,
Lighter of foot than cats.
I must have heard the bells, but more as air, as
        spicy wood,
Than bronze; as sun, as shade; as silence;
As contemplation, searching an unknown tongue.

Once More

The catkins and the starting cones,
The buds that hourly swell, and weep
Sweet gum from pain of so much pleasure;
Grass beginning, and the willow
Tops tempestuous with yellow;
Waterfall noise, and the wayfaring tree
Once more with rusty ram's heads on it,
Silly, erect, the ears stuck out—
Nothing is changed unless I am.
Here it all rises, not to be stopped;
Here it all comes, from so far back
The mind of a man cannot remember.
Let me not try. Let it all be.
It will—the wind, there—anyway.

May

All at once it is here.
But then it takes its time.
The best month is the longest,
Thank God: the slow smile,
Loving its own dearness
Daily, with delicate changes
As more and more is remembered
Of what again must be:
Spring turning to summer
And yet remaining spring;
Trees still transparent;
Leaves clear and green;
Everywhere flowers;
Ferns—look—in a ring;
And birds flying over
As if this were forever.

Birds in the Morning

Birds in the morning,
Before I rise:
Do they wake up slowly
As darkness dies?
Do they wish it were longer,
And close their eyes,
Then open them wider
And wider, with sighs?

I have listened, some mornings,
To their small notes,
And wondered if they too
Thought my thoughts.
Yet only a minute—
A clearing of throats—
Then to me and each other,
Thousands of shouts.

Down World and Up

The sound of water falling, out of sight,
Incessant, contradicts
This fernery as far as I can see,
This eager undergrowth
That yesterday was shorter in the half
Shade, half thrusting sun,
And months ago had no green top at all.
Here now it rises, rises,
Silently, heaving the moisture higher
That cataracts would waste.
Down world and up, water is fall, is fountain;
Water goes both ways; water
In deep woods never is certain which.

Wayfaring Tree

Under the broad leaves,
Her green ceiling,
A song sparrow sits,
Unaware of my feeling
This joy, this joy
That she comes again.
Five years it has been
Since our first meeting.

Or is she the same one?
How can I tell?
Unaware of my window
As ever. Still—
Joy, joy,
She is out there again.
Five years it has been
Since our first meeting.

She, or another one:
Why should I care?
But I do, I do,
I think she has seen me—
Joy, joy—
Again and again.
Five years it has been
Since our first meeting.

Tell Me How the Rain Arrives

Tell me how the rain arrives,
Grasses.
Make the sound that of all sounds
Most pleases.
Music's day is overdue,
And the night, too,
When all there is to hear is needle
Stitches
Sewing green to ground, and ground
By organ sound
To deepdown masses
Of thirsty sand and sunless rock—
O great rain, bless us.

King Wind

Of all the weathers wind is king.
Snow would not blow, nor rain beat,
Nor grasses ripple, nor trees break,
Except for the will of this blind thing
That neither is seen nor sees, but anyway
Comes, and anyway goes—from where
To where? Nobody knows.

I never am tired of thinking of him.
Even in sleep—but where is his bed?—
He dreams of filling the world again
With waves of water and walls of air
That neither can stop nor stand, but anyway
Rise, and anyway fall. So on
Forever. Motion is all.

I Mean Weather

When I say weather I mean
Weather. Not this eternal
Waiting for something to happen.
I mean the happening—wind
Of a sudden, thunder, and screams
Of lightning, and then of course
Rain: blasts of it, blearing
These windows, and what do I care
If it breaks a few? In a minute
The wind will stop, and the water
In straight-down streams will drum
On the dry ground all day,
All night, till the sound of it changes
To gurgling, and little rivers
Run together in puddles
And pools—oh, everywhere,
As if the earth had smiling
Eyes all over its body,
As maybe I do, I do.

Exodus

What if all four-footed things
Started to run and kept on running?
All in the same direction, too,
As if there were a wind that blew them.

But no wind. Only their wills;
Or one will, if even that;
More like a scent that lifted their heads,
More like a voice that called and called

Till all of them heard and had to go,
Faster and faster, as if they were stung.
But no sting. Only this having,
Desperate, to get there soon:

All together, if that might be,
The big, the little, the moose, the shrew,
Arriving in time—for what? And where?
Who would know, in the silence here?

Hunter and Hunted

One day there came to me out of the woods
A lily-white leopard, and laid in my hand
A lily-white dove he had bitten to death.

The dove was speckled with crimson blood,
And her head hung down, and I said to the
    leopard,
Why did you kill this beautiful bird?

He took it out of my hand again,
Sadly, and went back into the woods.
I had refused his wonderful gift.

If this was a dream, I have it still,
But the eyes of the leopard are what I remember.
Hunter and hunted: they broke my heart.

Indian Hunter

Forgive me, little antelope,
I kill you so that I may live;
Also my son; also his starving
Mother, whom I still can save
If only I can bring you down—
There—that arrow was my own—
Forgive me, little twitching thing
Of whom tonight we all will sing:

> One for three,
> And nothing wasted;
> On your smallest
> Bones we feasted.

> May you not be
> Too much missed,
> Youngest one
> That trotted last.

Wanting Two Worlds

Southwest of me
Two thousand miles—
Ah, could I ride
My memory there,
Arriving in sun,
The original one,
Drinking that air;

Southwest of here,
Too far for now,
The desert considers
Its endless self;
Sleeps and wakes—
Ah, if remembering
Were being there,

Ah, could I thin
Myself to that,
Becoming once more
The same as those shapes,
The blue, the brown—
Ah, if both those
And these were my own.

Will You, Won't You?

Cat in the cold, so eager to come in—
The door opens, and there is no more cat—
Where is he? On the best bed already.
How did he get there in no time at all?

Warm nights, he hesitates; retreats;
Advances; sniffs the threshold, rubs the jamb;
Goes again; returns; stretches his neck
To see what he knows will be there—nothing is
    strange—

Come in, come in! And so he does. But says:
Doors are final. Have to think them over.
In, out: which is better? Two
Minds about it—mine. Yours, a third.

Vain Advice

No, no, not birds.
Don't you understand?
Chipmunks, yes, and red squirrels;
Mice, too—there are millions.

No, no, not flyers,
Not singers; not slate-colored
Juncos or red-breasted nuthatches—
See, with the stripe at the eye?

Not chickadees—God!
No, no! Understand?
Beautiful green-eyed killer,
Look at me. Are you listening?

When the Wren Comes

When the wren comes—
From where?—
I rejoice.
That voice,
Pouring straight up as if to tear
Holes in the bright air,
Was what I missed.
Now here it is.
That tiny rage—
Yet there!
It wraps itself, I think, in joy—
Is how I know
Earth, heaven, and hell
Continue well.

Waving in Water

Waving in water—
Strong the stream—
Roots of red willow
Are not to be straightened,
Though current tries,

And the bodies of fishes,
Holding their places,
Equally ripple
As if they were elsewhere—
Pennants in wind—

And still the strong water
Works at the wavering
Yellow-green grasses;
Only dislodging
Last summer's leaves.

The Father Tree

There is a tree behind my house
That is so huge, hanging over—
And its roots, I have no doubt,
Tunnel under, tunnel under—

There is a great grey living thing
Above, beneath me, I might fear;
And so I do, in furious wind,
Or in midwinter when it cracks

And certain limbs that rub each other
Seem to say the time has come.
Yet it never has, I know;
Here we both are, big and little;

Here I am, in that vast lap,
Verily hugged by all those arms,
Verily resting on those knees
Deep underground that no one sees.

Midnight Music

Listen. There's the brook at last.
Hear it? No, that isn't wind,
It's water—too much water—no,
Enough, enough, and then more.

The sound of more was what we missed.
Imagine how it drowns the rocks
And tosses foam that night can't see.
But daylight will, and so must we.

Let's not be late. Let's get up now.
Those five dry years, this thirsty ground
Could drink it all before we come.
We'll give high water welcome home.

The Silent Birds

The silent birds of late summer,
When leaves hang heavy and song is over:
You hardly see them, tree to tree,
On trips so practical, so brief,
You wonder why they don't fly home;
And soon they will have, most of them.

Meanwhile, though, the ones that stay:
What are they doing, day by day,
Except forgetting their great time
When nests were building, and eggs came?
Or so it seems—the end deferred—
To someone not himself a bird.

Winter Calligraphy

The shapes of trees in heavy snow
Are how we know
At last their difference: one from another
And all things other.

Only trees—
Those, these—
Inscribe their names in white
Like day on night.

The solitary oak, with reach so vast,
The hemlocks, downcast—
See how they weep, those daughters of old kings,
For long lost things—

The black prince of birches, the urn
Of elm: see how in turn,
Grandchildren of sky,
They testify.

The Stove I Worship

The stove I worship lets me know
By waves of warmth and little sounds—
A snap, a settling—lets me hear
Its own content that I am near
After those icy days that were.

Could it have thought I wouldn't come?
But then I have, and here it is.
Identical as two can be,
We watch each other silently—
Except that crackling. That's for me.

Old Age Blues

What are those children so happy about?
You would think they knew,
But none of them does,
How the world no longer is what it was.

The blood has drained from most of its heart.
Only this part—
Those children there—
What can they be so blithe about?

Tell them, please, to be still, and wait.
It is getting late,
And the dark comes down.
This world will never be what it was.

Wait Till Then

"A dull day."
"And yet it is a day."
"What else? What could it be?"
"Why, nothing."
"Oh."
"You still don't understand, my child.
A dark day is so much more than no day—
Some day, none—"
"I see."
"But you don't see. With eyes as warm as yours,
As moist, as large—"
"And so I should see everything."
"Except nothing. Wait till then."
"When?"
"Forget, forget it. I must hold my tongue."
"No, tell me."
"Will not, cannot. Wait, I say,
Till any light at all is so much more
Than no light—oh, it blinds me, thinking of it,
As this day does, compared. I thank this day
For being. That's enough, that's fire and flame,
That's rockets bursting, that's one great
White ball of brightness breaking, that's
Lightning in the night—it shows the shapes
Of dear things still there—still there—"
"I see them."
"Not as I do, not as I do. Wait."
"Till when?"

Laly, Laly

There were two great trees
And a path between,
With a door at the end
That said "Come in,
My name is Laly.
Whoever you are,
Come gaily, gaily,
Without any fear."

"Who's Laly?" we said,
And didn't knock.
"Who's Laly?"—so loud,
Our voices came back.
Nobody knew
Who Laly was,
Or whether she listened
Inside the house.

Laly, Laly,
Whatever you said—
Forgive me truly—
We were afraid.
You shouldn't have told us
Not to be,
Laly, Laly,
So young were we.

First Letter

All capitals, and how they dance
On the paper, little and large
In a huddle, and some of the esses
Backwards. Many smudges; more
Erased than written; more
Afterthought than thought. The message
Nevertheless—I love you—wraps
The very voice of the writer, thin
And high and far away. Too far,
Too far. The breath falters, listening.

Who Knows?

In the far room four children's voices:
Birds, tossed in a wind, trying
To land, and failing; so up again,
Gay or furious—which? who knows?
Then silence. Such a silence. Even
Breathing has stopped. Or has it? No,
Waves of it against these walls.
They must have found the paper, must
Be writing—tongues out, heads
Close to the table top—must
Be printing their own sacred names,
Or drawing houses. Ah, but the birds:
Back again, in wind excitement,
Angry or loving—which? who knows?

Earliest Prime

So little time has gone,
And they are still so green,
You would not think these children
Had ever suffered change:
Had lost by any autumn
The least hue of spring.

Listen, though, and look.
They are not what they were.
Even so soon may glory
Depart. And be replaced.
Yet not without a difference
That catches at the breath.

Even so soon this prime,
Their earliest, is past.
Nor does fall grow familiar
Till its own end has come:
Till every hint of color
Subsides into snow.

For the Time Being

For the time being, and no more than that,
Even, possibly, not half so long,
There is this empty mountainside we live on,
And this old house that all but has a tongue
To tell us of the people who passed by,
And some of them turned in: society.

The road that stops here once went up and over,
And the high fields were cleared of trees, of stones.
Now walls in dark woods; they cannot remember
The feel of hands, even the latest ones,
So long ago it is since the last man
Walked there; find his footprints if you can.

Down here, though, all is open, or most is:
A wedge of green that keeps the wild away;
Or we do; it is not done by itself.
Eight meadows taper up till stone and tree
Close in for good; and near the apex of it,
The Bradford house that now we two inhabit.

How the place pleases us is no one's worry.
We do not say, even to each other,
How very well it does; how, as the seasons
Creep, we nod to every kind of weather:
The worst, the best, no matter; here we are,
And here it is, the country we prefer.

Elsewhere the world is changing; that we know,
And do not mind as long as this remains.
How long? No rumor tells. Meanwhile the wind
In winter, and in spring and fall the rains,
The evenings, short and long, with company
     coming,
Maybe—it could be a kind of dreaming,

An afterlife, before the time for that;
Not here and now at all, not anywhere.
Yet here it is, the place, the beautiful fields,
And here, certain as Saturday, both of us are.
As Sunday, too, as Monday; on which day
Comes David, who does all my chores for me.

John Bradford

John Bradford, who was buried on this place
Forever and forever and ago—
Is he the one I think is out there now,
Looking in? Such brightness,
Strangeness. John
Bradford, such a difference by day,
Too; you might come then. I know you won't.
Night is the time: a still night, like this one,
With no sounds from the barn. Have you been
    down there?
An odd thing: no horses,
Cows; and the pigpen smells
Of no pigs any more. No calves,
No colts. Have you a face, John
Bradford? Could I see you if I tried?
But then I won't. The window is for you:
For looking in, not out. If you have eyes.
Have you? Such a silence. John
Bradford, I am turning out the lights
And going up to bed, as you did once.
Forgive me, old
Man. Goodnight, goodnight.

Ghost Boy

He came down the old road
Where nobody lives now—
The houses are but bramble holes,
The lilacs have been shaded out—
He skipped over fallen limbs,
He whistled to the bright birds,
He came down the dead road
And said his name, I swear he did,
Was Chipman, which it couldn't be,
For never in a hundred years
Have any Chipmans been up there.
Chipman? No. But on he trotted,
Barefoot, in tattered pants,
His eyes wide open, looking
Left and right for something low,
Something that he had to see;
And stopped where the school was.
Nothing but a place now,
Nothing, even stones, there.
Nevertheless he turned in,
Took off his cap, and sat down—
And disappeared in sudden mist.
It cleared, but he was clean gone;
And still is, although I hear
Some days a bell ring,
Sometimes a pencil tap.

Jehu

Jehu the furious driver
Went like the wind that day—no, faster—
From Ramoth-Gilead west across the Jordan
All of the way to Jezreel, bringing
Death in a cloud of dust: death
To Joram, son of Ahab, who in his chariot
Fled, but Jehu's arrow overtook him;
Death then to Ahaziah, king of Judah;
And death to all of Ahab's house,
His seventy sons, his kinsmen and his friends,
His worshippers of Baal; death
To Jezebel, whose body the dogs ate;
Death everywhere that day and the next day,
And the next, until Elijah,
Waiting the bloody word, was satisfied
For Naboth, whose vineyard Ahab coveted,
For Naboth, whom Jezebel by false witness
Had moved the mob to stone; for Naboth,
Quiet man, who in his grave
Knew nothing of the wind and dust
This furious day when Jehu drove
His chariot all the way from Ramoth-Gilead,
Himself an arrow, aimed by Jehovah's wrath.

Psalms

Psalm 1

As far as the wings of his love unfold—
Where, oh, where have they not been heard
With the wind in their tips, the beating, beating?—

As far as the arms of his wrath can spread—
When, oh, when have they not been felt
By us the offenders, broken, bruised?—

As far as mercy can see in the dark—
When, oh, when have we not looked up
But only the milk-white moon was there?—

As wide as the world and wider—oh,
The reach of him takes my breath with trying.
When shall I cease and quiet my soul?

There is no end, there was no beginning.
As long as I live, the terror of him.
And the gentleness—ah, yes, the brooding.

He sings to me when I am sad.
His voice is old, but sweeter than new honey.
It comes from farther off than I can see.
It is not the world singing, it is he
That made it, and he makes it once again
As way down here I listen,
Listen, and am sad once more
With so much sweetness,
Sweetness—O, my Lord, how can I bear it?
Yet bear it, says the song, and so I do,
I bear it, all that sweetness, as he has
Forever, says the song he sings to me.

Psalm 3

Praise Orion and the Great Bear,
Praise icy Sirius so burning blue,
Praise the slow dawn, but then the razor rim
Of sun that in another hour
Cannot be looked at lest it blind you; praise
Mountain tops, praise valleys, praise the silver
Streams that circle towns; praise people's houses;
Praise sitting cats that wait for doors to open;
Praise running dogs; praise women, men;
Praise little boys who think their fathers perfect;
Praise fathers who believe their Father perfect;
Praise him because he is, because he has
His being where no eye, no ear can follow,
No mind say whence or whither,
Yet he is, and nothing else is
Save as witness to his wonder,
Save as hungering to praise him—
Let all things, then, great or little,
Praise him, praise him
Without end.

Where was I when the world was made?
Where am I now? What trees are these
That overhang me, and what waters lie
Off there for me to overlook?
What time is it, O Lord,
And am I late in your procession? Tell me,
Tell me my true name. Appear
And call me.
Such a silence.
I never should have asked. I shut my mouth
In shame. I should be proud
To be at all; and am; and shout for joy
That all things are that are, O maker of them
Now as in the beginning, now
As at the end. Is there to be an end?
I do not ask it, maker of each moment—
This one, this one—see? I hold my tongue.

Psalm 5

I will not cease to say your name
However many smile at me,
However many claim they know
You were not here before things were
Nor will be after—O, my Lord,
The lastingness, the lastingness.
It makes a newborn child of me
Who have white hairs; it shrinks the hills
Till nothing shows, as on that day
When the dry land appeared; it withers
Time, that then you planted, only to grow
As Jonah's gourd did till the worm
Wilted it. The lastingness—
I will not cease to sing of this
While I have voice, while all those fools
Deny it in their very hearts.

The great whale you made,
The polar bear, the golden eagle:
See how they die, my Lord, in air and water
Which also once you made. Save water,
Air, save world—remember, Sir,
The days of its creation—save it all,
Beginning now, let no more forms
Perish. For they do, you let them do—
Forgive me—and say nothing. Why,
Lord, do you not rage?
The lion, too, and the leopard—why,
O you that gave them life,
Do you not thunder, halting their destruction?
The steaming hippopotamus, the trumpeting
Elephant: those also, good my Lord,
Are worthy of your wrath. Why, then—
Forgive, forgive me,
But I ask.

Psalm 7

Let all men, Lord, see clearly
What you are beyond this world
Your plaything. Let their eyes and mine
Leap over what is near, is dark;
Let brightness be as on the first of days
It flamed above the firmament—
Your face, that no one since has seen.
And no one saw it then, alas;
Those eyes, forever open—none that looked
Has looked again, as we shall do if—
Lord, let us risk it
And be done.

How true are you, O Lord,
To your most faithful lovers?
How strictly do you heed their deep desires
They keep the world from knowing, but not you?
Oh, no, not you. But the world, then—
Was it for nothing that you made it thus?
Do you not pity them who need its love,
Its honor, when those blessings are denied?
When fame, that you call transitory,
A mushroom that will die on the third day,
A worm that turns and feeds upon itself—
So be it. Yet the world,
That is sole judge of this,
Mysteriously withholds
Or grants it, O my Lord, as you withhold
And grant your greater favor, grace.
Is there no likeness here? For I lack fame
And grieve therefor, I am cast down
As if by you. And yet not you, I know.
And yet men's praises—if there be a likeness,
Let them ring like chimes, your chimes,
At least, my distant Lord,
This little while.

Captain, you know my sins.
You kept the log; you cannot have forgotten
That sleeping at the wheel. We did not founder,
And yet I closed my eyes, and a wave came
So broadside, we shivered.
Master on sea, on land, you know my weakness:
Sloth, and a love of slumber;
Days wasted, beautiful deeds
Not done when I could have done them.
Or could I? Who can say? Breathe now
The truth upon me, even if it
Blasts me.
Now is the time, the midnight hour
When I am low,
Am longing to confess.
Or wait till I grow proud again, the memory
Of all this gone from me. If it be better thus,
Smite then. You are the swordsman,
I the receiver. As you will,
O, executioner with lifted arm.
My neck is bare.

Nothing matters, Lord, except
Your mind that is not matter. Nor is mine:
You tell me so and I believe you. Yet it fails
When body fails, and goes with that to death.
Or does it? You have never told me this.
The soul, you said, was free. But the labor-loving
Intellect: I think it tires at last.
And even in its prime, my Lord,
What did it do for you that needed doing?
Your thought that outstrips light—
No, no, for it does not race, it only waits
Till the red-eyed terrier comes round again—
Your thought that is not thought, but knowing,
As far surpasses mine as death does sleep;
And yet it is not death, except as matter
Dies in it, then lives again
As I do in your presence, O, my loved,
My loving Lord.

As near as the south wind on my cheek—
Nothing, I thought once, could lie closer,
But I was wrong, dear Lord, I was wrong—

As near as the lips of them I love—
Nothing, I said, could ever be sweeter,
But that was before I had tasted this—

As near as the blood in my own heart—
What more certainly at the center?
But something else is, wait till I tell you—

As near as the air that I displace
Yet some of it enters me—no, not that,
For it goes again, then more of it there—

You know, my Lord who is worlds away
Yet here, yet here where I have my being—
You know, that singeth—not I—this song.

By Mark Van Doren

POETRY

Mark Van Doren: 100 Poems
The Narrative Poems of Mark Van Doren
Collected and New Poems: 1924–1963
Collected Poems
Jonathan Gentry
A Winter Diary
Mortal Summer
The Mayfield Deer
The Seven Sleepers and Other Poems
New Poems
Spring Birth and Other Poems
Morning Worship and Other Poems
Selected Poems

DRAMA

The Last Days of Lincoln
Mark Van Doren: Three Plays

FICTION

Collected Stories, Volume 1
Collected Stories, Volume 2
Collected Stories, Volume 3
The Short Stories of Mark Van Doren
The Witch of Ramoth and Other Tales
Nobody Say a Word and Other Stories
Home with Hazel and Other Stories
The Transients
Windless Cabins
Tilda